LULU PRESS

Breathe

Living a Purposeful Life with Cystic Fibrosis

Jake Shavers

Inquiries to: jakeshavers@hotmail.com

Breathe: Living a Purposeful Life with Cystic Fibrosis ©, is the inspirational autobiography of Jake Shavers. At 41 years old, Jake Shavers is beating the odds. Born with Cystic Fibrosis, a genetic chronic disease that affects the lungs and digestive system, he bravely fights the debilitating illness. Given the statistics, he was not expected to live to see the age of 20. Even now, he has faced and conquered near-death experiences 5 times.

Against all odds, including a double lung transplant and a kidney transplant, Jake continues to thrive. His positive attitude and conviction in his faith gave him the strength and courage to compete in a half-marathon, exercise daily and give back through his work with children and adults facing similar situations. Jake attributes his success to his faith and knows he is here for a very special reason.

Credits: Roxanne Larcher, project manager, writing consultant and editor. Design by David Gore, D Gore Photos.

ISBN#: 978-1-304-68402-8

10 9 8 7 6 5 4 3 2 1

Table of Contents

Acknowledgements

Most books dedicate a section to acknowledging the people who made the book happen.

For me, the acknowledgements page is larger than writing this important work. It's about acknowledging the people who supported me, nurtured me and literally made it possible for me to live to see today.

It's about taking a moment to pause, thank and celebrate those who have made a lasting impact on my life. Please join me as I recognize those to whom I am deeply grateful and appreciate, with every fiber of my being...

- My Mom, whom I love with all my might, whose own love, strength and compassion know no bounds. Thank you for everything and for your amazing gift.

- Paul, my baby brother, whom I love. Paul has been with me through all the trying times. I know he always has my back.

- Elizabeth, my sister, whom I love so much and who has helped me throughout my life in so many ways.

- Uncle Mike for his love and for always being there in my life

- Paulie, Nicholas and Joshy, my nephews, whom I love very much. They provided me with energy and gave me the inspiration to keep trying when things got tough.

- Jennifer and Caitlin, my cousins, for their unconditional love.

- Mickie Tennyson, one of my mother's best friends, who prayed for me through all my trying times. I am eternally grateful for her.

- Ernest, Brad and Adam, my Atlanta family. Thanks for all the good times and always being there for all these years.

- My good friends and brothers for life: Rod Wilson, Mike Janiak, Mark Walter, Justin Rhodes, Mike Haddock and Damon Burrell.

- Carmen and Ari, whom I love very much and appreciate for bringing so much joy into my life

- And above all else, the Lord, for His strength, guidance and love. I bear witness that through Him, all things are possible.

Thank you. I love you.

A Word from Jake

When I look back at my life, it is crystal clear that God has a special purpose for me. I was diagnosed with Cystic Fibrosis at 5 years old.

- I was not supposed to live past 20, yet I am now 41 years old.

- Most people who need organ transplants typically need only one organ replaced; I faced two organ transplants – double lung and kidney, both of which I received.

- When others have had to wait years for an organ donor (if one arrives at all), I was blessed to receive a call and have my first organ transplant within 3 days of being on the list.

These examples and countless others have manifested the truth that God lives and that I am here on this planet for a reason.

I believe it is to help someone – whether they are living with a serious disease such as Cystic Fibrosis or have a loved one with a medical condition, or are facing hardships and challenges of a different nature – my goal in life is to help just one person have faith and courage to triumphantly face the unknown head on and overcome.

That is my main goal in writing this book – to provide inspiration, knowledge and faith that God does live … that if we, as fragile human beings, place our trust and faith in Him, we can overcome and can lead a life of purpose and meaning, despite any unhappy circumstance. If I can help just one person, then I have served God's purpose.

May my story help you find the light you seek.

The Early Years

I was born on Tuesday, August 15, 1972 in Lansing, Wayne County, Michigan to a family with four siblings and five half-brothers and sisters. Mom was the anchor of the family; she loved all of us with her whole soul and taught us strong values of family first and the belief that we could do anything if we just tried. My father was rarely around; he was busy with work and other life experiences. But Mom was always there. She was my Rock of Gibraltar, the foundation of our family.

Grandma and my grandfather, whom I called Papa, were very involved in our family life. I remember great times at their house, especially discovering my love of the great American pastime. Both Papa and Grandma loved baseball. Grandma bought me my first glove when I was 4 years old and we'd play catch in the afternoon in their huge backyard.

Papa would sit on the porch and watch us, cheering me on as I learned the ins and outs of the game. I joined local baseball teams and my whole family would come to watch my games. I'm proud to say that all the baseball teams I played on went on to win championships.

Top: 4 years old with my first glove

Bottom: 10 years old, 5th place in national bowling tournament

8 years old, in love with the great American past time

11 years old, All Star Team

11 years old, in our team uniforms

12 years old, bowling team

In the summertime in Michigan, Papa made swimming pools for my brother and me. He'd find huge industrial garbage cans and scrub them clean. Then, he'd fill them with ice-cold water from the water hose and we'd jump in and swim! It was the best way to cool down after a good game of catch with Grandma.

We loved swimming a lot. In fact, some of my earliest childhood memories were swimming in the garbage cans at Papa's – and taking trips twice a week to the Batavia Quarry. It's actually called the Harold Hall Quarry Beach and its part of the Batavia Park District. It's 60,000 square feet of fun! My friends and I knew each foot of the quarry beach like the back of our hands. We played on the playground, dove in head first in the diving area and after a hard day of play, enjoyed relaxing at the picnic tables where we filled our bellies until content.

Like most young boys, I loved sports. My first love was, and still is, baseball – most probably because of Grandma and Papa's influence. My favorite all-around baseball player was Dwight Gooden, who played for the Mets. Basketball is also a sport I enjoyed playing. I loved watching any team play. I even loved bowling!

I'd play sports with my friends all afternoon. We'd fill a cooler with snacks and sodas and play until the sun came down and Mom made me come home and eat. These are great memories and great times.

Even though I was very active as a child, I was also really sick. I always felt tired and never felt very well. And I was small for my age. During my early years, Mom took me to see many doctors and many specialists for tests and diagnostics, but we never found an answer. One doctor even gave me 100 shots in each leg in one day as part of a battery of allergy tests. I was only 4 years old at the time and remember that it really hurt – and not just physically in my legs. My little mind was confused because my body hurt all the time and I didn't know why I had to take all of these tests just to see Mom look so disappointed after. I remember hearing doctors use the phrase "failure to thrive" and that made Mom the saddest of all because we didn't know why I was not able to thrive.

I loved sports, especially baseball. From the time I could walk, I would find a ball to throw and a bat. I'd hit the ball and then then chase after it. But my chasing wasn't easy, because I couldn't breathe very well. My lungs would fill up and I would cough so hard it hurt, trying to make it easier to breath. I always wondered why it hurt me so much and not the other kids. Why was I so different? But it didn't take away my love of baseball and I still played.

An Answer

Sometime shortly before I turned 5 years old, Mom found a doctor who asked her a weird question. She asked Mom if, when Mom kissed me, my skin tasted salty. She said yes – and that was when I was given a Sweat Test, a special assessment that measures the level of salt in your sweat. When the results came in, we had our answer as to why I was not like the other kids.

I was formally diagnosed with Cystic Fibrosis, or CF. Symptoms of CF include frequent coughing with phlegm, severe lung infections like bronchitis and pneumonia, shortness of breath and poor growth and weight gain, even with a strong appetite – in other words, failure to thrive even when you're doing the right things.

We learned that CF is a genetic disease where both parents are carriers of a defective CF gene. Sometimes the parents can be carriers of the defective gene without having the disease themselves and if one child has CF, it's a good idea to test all of the children, which Mom did. We found out that my younger sister, Evelyn, who was five years younger than me, also had CF. Sharing a very serious illness made me and "Pooky," as we called Evelyn, very close.

Me (11 years old), Papa, Pooky and Paul

You might think that Mom's reaction would be one of guilt or to be over protective of Evelyn and me – but it was quite the opposite. Mom knew that genetics were not in our control and she also knew that if she were to be overprotective of us, it would rob us of the chance to really live and experience the many opportunities that life has to offer.

I was so thankful that Mom never treated us any differently. I didn't want special treatment because of the illness; I wanted to be normal, to live and to play sports and to have fun. I had the spirit of any normal little boy, who wanted to live life to its fullest. Back in the 70's, medical statistics showed that most children with CF lived to about 18 years old.

Once I was diagnosed with CF and began treatment, my health improved dramatically. I took my prescription powder when I ate, started getting chest physical therapy to clear my lungs and drain them so I could breathe better and learned how to be strong.

It was tough being so different from the other kids. Many times I felt angry, depressed and bitter because I was smaller than the other boys, couldn't run fast without having to stop and I had to do so many medical things that other kids my age didn't have to do.

A Defining Moment

When I was seven years old, Mom sent me to Summer CF Camp. It was a special camp designed specifically for children fighting CF. From the moment I stepped onto the campground, I knew I was someplace special. There were other kids, just like me, who had to wake up in the morning and clear their airways, feed through a tube and be careful to take the right medicines when eating. And what was more, there was another black child there – I am half-black and CF is typically found in white people much more than in black people. To find someone who not only faced the same physical challenges as I did, but looked like me as well, was exhilarating.

For once in my life, I felt normal.

My fellow campers and I started our days by meeting at the bank of a hill. We'd watch the sunrise and the sunset as we'd pair up and do chest palpitations with each other. Being with people who did the same things to stay healthy was cool.

I loved dining hall time. We'd have different contests – like the one where there was a wooden Popsicle stick hidden on the underside of a chair. Whoever sat in the chair had to do what the camp wanted them to do – like sing a silly song in front of everyone – or they'd face being thrown in the lake by the rest of the campers with whatever clothes were on.

Being together with other kids was awesome. Of course, there were organized activities which we enjoyed but our real focus was hanging out together, talking and getting to know each other - sharing our joys, our dreams and our fears. It was like a week-long sleepover with cool things to do during the day.

My brothers and sisters went to camp with me. They liked camp well enough, but I fell in love with it. In fact, camp was so important to me, I promised myself I was going every year.

It became one of the ways I defined myself as a person, so much so that still to this day, I am an experienced volunteer camp counselor.

Pre-Teens

Despite the physical challenges of CF, I was a very active kid. I loved sports – my absolute favorite was baseball, followed by a close second of bowling. When I played ball, the thrill of hitting the ball and making a home run called to me. I played on baseball leagues, loving the camaraderie and the sport itself.

As each birthday passed, I became more and more physically fragile. I was smaller than the rest of my peers and weighed considerable less, a symptom of CF. Even though I was still athletic and participated in sports as much as I could, I felt as though my physical being was dying a very slow death.

In fact, my body was starting to give out. I was beginning to die.

It's hard to explain how I knew it, but I did. Imagine, for a moment, tune into your breathing. Take a deep breath and feel your lungs expand. Now, exhale and feel your lungs contract. Do it again and bring your focus to the muscles in your back surrounding your lungs. As you take in the oxygen, if you really concentrate, you can feel the back muscles support your breathing. Now, think back to the last time you had a cold or a sinus infection. You know how you can feel the illness, sensing how your muscles and cells are fighting the infection? It's like that ... but more intense, minus the feeling of getting better, only getting worse. And when your body can't get the air it needs to bring fresh life in, you can feel your limbs get weak, your muscles slow down and you feel your life force become less and less.

It's scary for anyone, but especially scary for a young child.

Turning Point

I was 11 years old and weighed about 50 lbs when I came to an important crossroad in my life. One day, my father, who at the time was living in Georgia while I was living in Chicago, was watching CNN. He saw a news segment about a ground-breaking study sponsored by Vanderbilt University in Tennessee that focused on weight gain through feeding tubes. My father was so hopeful that he sent money to my Mom and told her to enroll both me and Evelyn in the study.

Mom accepted the money, and filled out the application forms for us. Shortly after receiving our request, Vanderbilt accepted both of us into the study. As soon as the news came in, Mom made the arrangements and we traveled to Tennessee to be admitted.

We stayed in the same room together. I was committed to doing whatever it took to finish the study and get my health back. I wanted to play sports again with my friends without losing my breath. I wanted to hit the ball out of the park and run all the bases to score that homerun.

Evelyn was younger than me, about five years younger. Although she was excited about the study at the beginning, I don't think that at her age, she understood what the study meant and how much it would demand from her.

It was a physically challenging process. We were taught how to use a tube to feed ourselves through a tube. The tube, called a nasogastric tube, was inserted through the nose and then traveled the course of the throat until reaching the stomach. Then, once it was in place, nutrition was pumped into the stomach so that the digestive process could take place.

Inserting a tube in your nostrils can be uncomfortable, and as you can imagine, when the tube goes down the throat, it's painful and can make you gag. I faced the physical challenges head-on, learning how to relax my throat muscles and work with my body to accept the tube and the food.

But Evelyn could not. She tried really hard, but couldn't do it herself. The nurses came in to help her and it was even worse. She'd scream in pain, ripping my heart out. I begged the staff not to hurt her. I tried to protect her from the pain. Mom was there, crying in helplessness, tormented by seeing her daughter in pain.

We had to feed ourselves morning and night and each time, it was the same for Evelyn.

It took me about six times before I finally mastered the feeding process.

But it never worked for Evelyn. She was the opposite of me. Whether it was due to her age or for other reasons, she didn't have the mental capacity to deal with the physical and emotional pressure associated with the study. After only two attempts at the feeding, she gave up and stopped. She was so smart and had so many different talents in her life … but when it came to this study, she just did not have the drive and energy in her to deal with it.

Evelyn was such a good person with a good heart and a sensitive soul, but she struggled to take her medicine on a regular basis and consistently take the necessary steps to stay healthy. I remember trying to support her and encourage her to do the right things to take care of herself; sometimes, she followed my lead and other times, she got caught up in the joy of life that the medical side took a back seat.

Pooky struggled with CF.

She dropped out of the study, but I kept on.

I continued to press on with the program. I had to give up all solid foods and rely on only the tube feedings. Very quickly, I started to see and feel *real* results. My muscles became stronger. I had more energy. I slept better.

But things did not go completely smooth.

Nearly two weeks into the study, I got really sick. I came down with an infection and lost the ground I had gained in the beginning. I was hot with fever and I couldn't keep much of the nutrition down, and what little I could keep inside, was used by my body to fight the infection. I had to stop the study for a couple of days so that I could take antibiotics and get over the infection.

Mom and my brother sat with me while I was fighting the infection. They encouraged me, held my hand and helped me keep the courage to fight the infection, get well and get back in the study. I'd responded so well to the treatment, it was clear that the feedings could be a major tool for me in living a good life with my CF disease.

I kept fighting and I did get better. I was able to complete the study and with my newfound knowledge, I continued with the nasogastric tube feeding protocol.

Time continued and I started to gain a lot of weight, getting and feeling stronger as the days went on. My health improved and I felt … *and lived* … the difference of getting proper nutrition to my body. The experience rejuvenated me and reinforced my commitment to do whatever it took to make me healthy and at least feel normal, to be able to do everyday things like other kids and to continue to play baseball.

In fact, I continue tube feedings to this day to maintain my health.

The experience also taught me that my success and my health truly is a question of mind over matter. I found a determined strength within that I didn't realize I had – I knew without a doubt that I would never let my illness own me or run me, that I would and could do anything and everything to be strong – and my body would obey. I **FOCUSED**. I witnessed the reaction when I fully committed to my health and saw the changes that took place.

I promised myself that I would place my health first and foremost.

The Teens (13-19 years old)

Family life took a turn during my teens. Like every teenager, I went to after school games, enjoyed hanging out with my friends and basically had a good time. My best friend's name was Rod. He and I were inseparable. We played sports together, did homework together and enjoyed the fun and mischievousness part and parcel of being a teenaged boy. I maintained my involvement with CF Camp. My parents didn't really push me to do well in school; as long as I didn't fail a class, they were happy and I was content with that.

When I was in the 7th grade, I was bowling in Saturday leagues and this kid came up to me. He said there were two guys that went to his school and looked exactly like me, and shared my same last name. He asked me if they were my brother and I told him he was crazy, that he knew my brother, Paul and that was the only brother I had. The kid was really adamant though, and insisted that they were my brothers. Something inside of me clicked and something didn't feel right. I knew deep within that the question needed an answer.

I went home and told Mom about the conversation. I asked her point blank, "Do I have any other brothers that I don't know about?" She looked at me and broke down crying. She said that yes, I did in fact have two brothers, Thor and Brant, and she never told me about them. I never knew they existed.

She explained that they were my fathers' children from another woman and asked me to forgive her for not telling me, which of course I did. I was in my early teens and while I could not understand the depths of my Mom's pain, I realized that Mom didn't keep the truth from me with the intention of hurting me; she did so to protect her children and of course, to protect herself from the pain of my father's betrayal of her love.

Although I knew about Thor and Brant, we didn't meet until a couple of years later.

A major change happened when I was a freshman in high school. After many years of living apart, my father came back to our lives for good and everything changed at home.

When I was younger, my father didn't live with us. He lived in Georgia for the most part, and I didn't see very much of him. Although he would visit once every three or four months, his work was in Georgia and that's where he stayed emotionally, even when he'd come to visit.

One time, for about two years, my father was not around. He was gone. We didn't hear from him or see him at all. We didn't know if he was dead or alive. Then, one day without any notice, he just showed up and walked back in the door, alive. Surprisingly, Mom let him back into our lives.

Before then, Mom managed the household with a nice balance of fun, love and the discipline required for raising me and my brother and sister. She had confidence and looked for the positive in life. She took us everywhere as a family. We had such a good time.

But when my father was back in the picture full time, his negativity and need for control eroded our joy.

He was mentally abusive and there was so much negativity from him that it was ridiculous. Each day was filled with arguing and fighting. If there wasn't something obvious to be upset about, then he'd find something to get upset about and we'd bear the brunt of his anger. He was a control freak, making my mother submit to his will.

It was his way or the highway and we all knew it - especially Mom. She had married my father, who was nineteen years older than her, when only 19 years old herself. You can imagine the resistance her family gave her for that decision. To compound the situation, Mom is white and my father is black. An interracial marriage in the late 70's, and even to some extent today, is difficult. Mom had three children back to back and her fourth child a year later. In her wildest dreams, perhaps she longed for an escape. But she didn't want to leave my father and put up with people saying, "I told you so." It takes a lot of mental power out of you to survive an abusive situation and I know she did her best to maintain the family … at the expense of herself.

That same year, Thor and Brant came to live with us in Aurora. My mom was really good about having them come to live with us on a permanent basis. I have to hand it to her – it takes a very strong woman to welcome another woman's children born from her husband's infidelity into her home with open arms. But Mom did. She never treated Thor or Brant any different from the rest of us. She always took care of all of us and raised us to the best of her ability. She never wavered in her integrity and commitment to be the best mother she could, despite the circumstance.

We never had much money before and now, with my father back in the picture, the family economics had a downturn. He gambled a lot and continued womanizing. He didn't have a steady job. What little money we had, he spent. There were eight of us and Mom was working herself to death to keep the roof over our head. Bills piled up, financial stress was constant and sometimes it felt like we were drowning. We lived in a mental and financial prison.

My health issues became even more apparent. I wasn't growing and keeping up physically with other boys my age. I was still weaker, still smaller than and not as fast as my teammates. I was still playing my beloved baseball, but my coach made me feel that I was too little and not good enough to be a major player on the team. I vividly remember the day he said that to me. I was hurt to the core – baseball was my everything and my coach, the one who was supposed to believe in me as a player, didn't have faith in my ability to hold my own. I felt like my health was holding me back. I wanted so badly to be normal – to not have to worry about my lungs filling with mucus, to breathe fully and deeply and be like everyone else. I continued doing everything I could to be normal – the daily tube feedings, taking medicine, being active.

In the depths of my despair, I began to develop a strong positive mental drive. I never shared my illness with anyone unless it was absolutely necessary. I found that when I did tell people about my condition, things changed. Typically, before someone knew I had CF, they treated me the same as everyone else. But as soon as they found out about it, more often than not, they became cautious for my health and even worse, afraid they might catch CF from me. And sometimes, like in the heartbreaking case of my baseball coach, knowing I had CF made some people doubt I could ever be more than what their own fears and doubts.

During my final years of high school, Evelyn got really sick. The CF started to gain momentum with her, sapping her strength and depleting her ability to breathe. As I helplessly watched her health diminish, I wished with all my might that I could take away her pain and suffering. If only God would let me take her sickness on and relieve her from her misery, I could handle it. I was the strong one. But one of life's hardest lessons was learned – no matter how hard you wish for something, sometimes, it just doesn't happen.

Evelyn went to the hospital for what would be the last time. Mom and my father talked with the doctors and decided to bring her home. They stopped giving her treatment and I'm not sure, but I think they decided to let her die at home, surrounded by her family, instead of in the hospital.

We lost Evelyn when she was only 13 years old.

As I look back now, I question how my sister could have passed away. Family life was chaotic, to say the best, and I think it greatly affected her spirit. While I was headstrong and didn't let the family dynamics consume me, Evelyn was deeply sensitive and internalized the disharmony. I strongly believe she was not allowed to get the care she needed. I don't have all the information that my parents relied on to make the decision for Evelyn to come home, so I can't say whether or not I would have done the same thing if I were in their shoes. But I can say that I am left with several unanswered questions.

When she died, I was filled with sadness and despair … and fear. It was the first time I realized I could die from my illness. This new knowledge changed my outlook – I started to lose sight of goals and lost a little of my drive. I fell into a hole of self-pity and anger. Why did it have to be me that had this illness? Why? Not that I wished any harm on others, but I often times remember thinking, "Why couldn't it have been someone else who had CF? Why me, God? Why me?"

The anger and injustice of it all consumed me. I became nonchalant about life, embracing the attitude of 'when it's my time to die, it's my time to die.'

My anger continued and my health deteriorated as well. I started going into the hospital more frequently during this period of my life – and started realizing the direct connection between my mental attitude and my physical being. I began to feel the real effects of my illness and all that went along with the disease. I maintained my commitment to being athletic, staying active and being as strong mentally as possible … but I no longer believed I had a purpose in life, nor did I believe in a God who could allow me to be so ill and take my sister away so young. I ignored what my life had in store for me.

At the end of this chapter in my life, I had no idea how my life would turn out or whether I would even make it.

I felt so alone.

But in the darkness, God whispered.

Young Adulthood (20-30 years)

They say everything changes – that if there's good, hold onto the memories because soon there will be challenges; when there's bad, hold on to faith that things will get better. I believe that and know it's true.

I had to distance myself from my family. The negativity had become unbearable and I knew I had to get out of the chaos. I moved to Atlanta when I was 22 years old and started going to the CF camp of Georgia. It was around this same time that I met my first wife, Tammy.

I continued to work out and do what I could to be healthy. But I was still depressed, even with the change in scenery. The emotional stress associated with the move to GA caught up with me, as did the heartbreak of losing my sister, and the family dynamics of the past several years continued to haunt me.

I didn't know what I was going to do or where life was taking me. I had no direction. I felt trapped. Although my focus was still on being healthy, my ego prevented me from seeing that the greatest gift I was blessed with was my life.

My visits to the hospital became more and more frequent. It was during my hospital visits that I met my first wife. Her name was Tammy and she was my nurse. We met during one of my routine visits and became friends. I started looking forward to seeing her when I knew it was time to go the hospital and she always seemed happy to see me.

As our friendship developed, we started calling each other. I remember that we hadn't talked for about six weeks when all of a sudden, I realized I missed her. So, I called her and she said she missed me too. We both recognized the conflict of interest with her being my nurse and me being a patient at her place of employment, so she quickly asked to be transferred off my case and we started dating in earnest.

I was no longer alone.

We were married when I was 23. The wedding was large – we had about 200 people in attendance. We got married in the church and then had a beautiful reception. I wore a tux and Tammy looked so amazing in her white wedding gown. I loved her with my entire heart and she loved me. It felt like I had finally reached a calm point in my life – I was actually living somewhat of a normal life, at least what normal meant to me.

Tammy and I settled into married life. We enjoyed normal day to day experiences like dinner at the family table, nights snuggled next to each other on the couch watching movies and other things that happy, married couples do together.

Even with my new bride and my newfound happiness, my visits to the hospital were frequent. In fact, we both started noticing that I was in the hospital more often than not. But my wife was always there when I needed her. Tammy stood by my side and took care of me, honoring her wedding vows to stand beside me in sickness and in health.

Tammy and I talked about having children. People who have CF are genetic carriers for passing the illness to their children. The way it works is that both parents have to either have the CF gene or be a carrier in order for the disability to pass through the blood line. We didn't know if Tammy was a carrier or not, but of course, we knew I was carrier.

I did a lot of soul searching and looked back at my life. When I thought about my experiences of living life with CF and all of the sickness, the medical visits, the treatments, and the pain – I knew I could never do that to another human being. I decided that I did not want to have children, but Tammy's desire to have children remained.

That didn't mean children were out of the picture for me. Memories of how important camp was to me when I was growing up spurred me on to become a counselor for the Cystic Fibrosis Camp of Georgia. I loved helping kids. It was so inspiring to see the hope in children's eyes when they realized they could have a life even if they were sick, when they see that life doesn't stop because they have an illness. Their joy and innocence inspired me and renewed my hope and joy as well.

My brother, Paul, and I grew very close. Gone were the days from our childhood of sibling rivalry and competition for Mom's attention, replaced with a deep brotherly love and a solid friendship. We spent hours together, talking, playing sports together and watching the games. It was great.

My commitment to being as healthy and strong as possible remained steadfast. Although my outlook was still "when it's my time to go, it's my time to go", I worked out on a regular, consistent basis with a routine well balanced with cardio, weight lifting for strength training and stretching for flexibility while continuing the nightly tube feedings.

I continued working as a Camp Counselor. Times changed and with budget cuts, specialized camps dedicated to a specific condition like CF lost funding to more diversified and inclusive camps catering to a wider population. Over the course of time, Cystic Fibrosis Camp of Georgia fell victim and closed its doors forever. It was a very sad day for me when I heard the news, but I had faith that other opportunities would arise and I would be able to continue my work as a camp counselor.

I was fortunate to find Camp Twin Lakes, a camp for kids with different illnesses including CF, as well as mental and physical disabilities. I was hired on to the team and continued my work as a Camp Counselor. It was important to me to find work doing my life passion; I knew in my heart that being a counselor and working with kids was my calling. It was my chance to give back and be a force for positive change.

I made a difference – I gave hope and inspiration to children by showing them, through my living example, that it is possible to live a full, purposeful life despite the physical, emotional and social challenges. The secret was – and is – a positive, focused mental outlook and a willingness to do whatever it takes to be as healthy and strong as possible.

I spent four of the best years of my life at Camp Twin Lakes. To this day, I still keep in touch with many of the campers and share their triumphs and successes.

1997, as a Counselor at CF camp

2001, my first year as a counselor at Camp Twin Lakes

2004, with some of my campers

Working at camp, all summer long

23 years old, Ribbon Cutting at the new CF Center, Atlanta GA

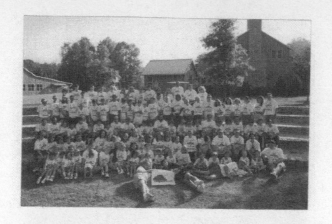

Summer Camp in Atlanta GA

~"To a great friend and a person who I care and ♥ very much"~

Oh wow ♥ I never thought that I would get to write you a letter again and actually be able to give it to you....(there go the tears :) Man I don't know where to start ?

The first thing that "POPS" into my mind would be summer 2001.... that is a summer I will never forget. That was when I was blessed by meeting my other Big Brother. I met you on a "hey... how are ya" bases @ Big ♥...
Then came ☼ I made it a point to say hey to you & annoy you more when I saw ya. (Got crap from the girls in the cabin cause they thought I liked ya... But hey you are cute ;)

So my 3rd week started, that was a fun even though you threw me in the pool. Yeah I still remember that. But all in all thoes were GREAT times ! The summer of 2002 came and yeah that was very different & interesting. Did not get to see you Before I left ☼, because someone was in guess where.... Bed♥. So the

31

time came to say c~ya later for the summer. But never in my wildest dreams would I think you would not be there in 2003? But yeah it happened. Boy I came and was like "where is Jake?" and was told you were not there. I knew something was up cause I had not seen you at Teen Retreats either. I then thought you were gone... I know I have told you before but from the time that we traded necklaces until.... I have always worn it. Except for prom... mom wouldn't let me. I would (and still do) look at our picture, your name tag, and the necklace and it reminded me of all the fun times we had...
I cannot even start to put into words how much

you have impacted my life? I want you to know and realize that I do consider you a "Big Brother" and always will... Hell, I have to look up to you in more than one way. Your strength is so amazing and at times is what keeps me going when I feel like giving up. But here is to a AWESOME summer of 2004 Thanks for helping to make this summer filled with the most amazing memories!

Thanks Big Brother.

P.S. How am I Suppose to call w/o your #?

Luv ya bunches
★ NMN

A wonderful card from a special Cancer Camp camper. She came to camp the four years I worked at Twin Lakes. We became very close friends.

Halfway through the second summer at Camp Twin Lakes, I developed a sinus infection that really kicked me. While something as simple as a sinus infection may not seem like a big threat, to someone with CF, it is – and was – a major health concern. I was not able to recover from the infection and my health quickly started to go downhill.

One again, I found myself spending more time in the hospital than I did at home.

As my illness progressed, the surgeries increased and I endured more and more procedures. This vicious cycle increased in speed – surgery, followed by a mini-recovery, only to get sick again and then have another procedure, then another surgery, then recover … it went on and on. My life went from somewhat normal, with conversations about athletics and sports, to revolving around medical routines, doctor visits, what new medications were working and what ones were not.

Romance became an afterthought, if it was even a thought. Before, Tammy and I loved to travel – sometimes, we'd grab a bag and go on a spur of the moment road trip. Those memories drifted to the far corners of our minds and instead, our conversations were exclusively dedicated to CF and my illness. I still held fast to the belief that when it was my time to go, it was my time to go. I failed to look beyond that belief or even to consider 'what if' and 'what else.'

I realize now that without a conscious commitment and promise to yourself and the one you love, it's easy to fall into bigger and bigger ruts. If I can offer one nugget of relationship advice, I'd urge you to keep the big picture of life and love in mind, even when fighting the deep details of any circumstance. It's important.

There were some really tough moments. My will to battle this sickness was there, but sometimes my flesh was weak. At times, it seemed as though I became an outside observer when I underwent the procedures. I watched myself go through the medical routines and began to notice that no matter what was thrown at me, I could handle it and I kept on.

My body started to shut down completely. I could not walk from room to room without completely losing my breath; eventually, I lost my strength and required oxygen 24 hours a day just to subsist.

As my health deteriorated, my doctors and medical team started talking to me about considering a lung transplant. I immediately rejected all the discussions, ignoring their advice and just keeping on as best as I could. I put the idea out of my mind.

Even with the oxygen tanks, I continued to work out. I promised myself that I would not let my illness get the best of me. I maintained a positive mental attitude and accomplished as much as I could each and every day.

Looking back now, I can see that a large part of me was in denial about how sick I really was. But I can also see that a transformation was taking place. I kept working out, despite the challenge of needing oxygen tanks to exist, and that's when working out became more than just a physical act. It became symbolic of the connection between my mind, body and soul. It was *the* way to train my mind to maintain a single focus; to physically and – more importantly – mentally prepare for the battles I faced at that instant in time – and for the rest of my life.

It took every ounce within me to fight – I poured my heart, body and soul into surviving and I clung to my health with a vice-like grip.

Most of that six to nine month period in my life is a blur to me now. It feels as though I was in a haze, like a time warp, but it is a calm feeling. I recall being at peace and knowing, at the soul level, that things would work out – and even when the darkest hours threatened me, things *always* worked out.

God's whisper became louder. I started to hear … I started to listen to the soft voice inside my heart. My belief became stronger. I discovered I was not alone, as I once thought. The Lord was in my life, shining His almighty light and love on my heart, giving me the strength I needed to continue.

Soon, His whisper could no longer be denied.

My Real Birthday

In 2002, I approached my 30th birthday on August 15th. On the eve of the celebration of my birth, I was in the final stages of dying.

I gradually accepted that I was not much longer for this world and my life would soon be over. When we are faced with our own mortality, many discussions with God take place. It's part of our human nature to seek solace and to find answers to our many questions. I began to pray to Him to please take me, if it was my time and His will, so that I would not have to suffer and bear the pain any longer. I wanted to rest. I needed peace.

Tammy, however, was a fighter and she wasn't giving up so easily. I faced each day with Tammy at my side. I leaned on her will to fight and each day, did what was necessary to make it through the 24 hours. She gave me strength and she gave me a voice – for a lot of things going on in my life, I spoke through her. She protected me, she helped me make decisions and she gave me the strength to continue.

One night, I was admitted to the hospital. As I lay in the hospital bed, I felt myself slipping away. My life force grew weak and frail. I was terrified.

My soul cried out - **I do not want to die**.

At death's door, it became clear.

I needed more time on this earth to live my purpose and to give back. I resolved to hang in, clinging to life by a thread, and I prayed with all my might.

It was a breaking point. It was the lowest I had fallen and I knew I could not give up.

God heard my cries and I was blessed with another day of life.

I immediately called my doctors in and told them that I was ready for the lung transplant.

It was time.

When I spoke the words to my medical team, their response was supportive – but realistic.

There are many factors to take into account when it comes to organ transplants. From a donor standpoint, the person who is donating the organs has to be a physical match to the recipient. A match is when there are enough biological and medical similarities, like the blood type and size of chest, for the person receiving the organ to accept and not reject the new organs. A big concern was my rare blood type, AB positive.

I also had to accept that even with a successful double lung transplant, CF does not go away. There is no cure for CF. The cystic fibrosis still lives in the pancreas, sweat glands, intestines, reproductive system and sinuses. I would still live with the disease. But at least, I would *live* with the disease I had known all my life.

My physical health was also of great concern to my doctors. I was dying, in the last stages of life, and my medical team did not know if I had passed the point of no return.

Time was also a big concern. Often times, people who are placed on the waiting list for organs spend years waiting for their turn. I did not have the luxury of more than a few weeks, at best.

It seemed like from the get-go, the odds were stacked against me.

Despite my fear and anxiety, I felt a calm peace and knew deep within that all would be okay.

My doctors and I had a lengthy discussion. I acknowledged the risks and also firmly stated my resolve to be strong enough to receive the lungs. The team listened to me and promised me they would do everything in their power to get me ready and approved to be on the wait list for a lung transplant

Lung transplants are officially known as pulmonary transplantation. It is a surgical procedure where lungs are taken from someone who just died (known as the donor) and placed into the body of the person who needs the organ(s). There are several types of lung transplants: heart-lung, lobe, single-lung and double-lung procedure.

I had to have a double lung transplant.

A double-lung transplant is the most common type of procedure undergone by people who live with CF. This surgery is where both lungs are replaced and the lungs can come from either one or two donors. The reason that CF patients need the double lung transplant is because the cystic fibrosis bacterium is present in both lungs. If only one lung is replaced with a normal, healthy lung, the patient runs the risk of CF bacteria from the unhealthy lung colonizing in the new, healthy lung and infecting the newly transplanted organ.

My doctors started me on the protocol to be evaluated for the transplant. There was a battery of tests that I had to take. I was fortunate enough to have access to the first round of tests at the hospital in which I was staying, North Side Hospital.

We finished the evaluation and began the waiting game of finding out the results. My doctors did not have a positive outlook on me passing the tests.

But I started to look at my life in chapters, segmenting the different challenges and battles into separate events. Each time I conquered one challenge, mentally checked the victory in my mind, celebrated for a moment and then left the challenge in the past and moved to the next chapter.

My evaluation tests were no exception. I finished at North Side, and then moved to the second battery of tests at the Medical Center at University of Alabama, Birmingham (UAB). I was admitted to UAB and started the tests, successfully completing all but one of the evaluations.

The last evaluation was the physical fitness test. I was so sick and so weak that I was scared, afraid I would not have the physical strength to perform the test, to make it to the end.

And the reality was that the consequence of not being able to pass the physical fitness test was literally a death sentence.

I prayed to God for His strength with all my might.

I used my mind to visualize, creating a laser-like focus. I watched myself successfully tackle any and every physical test I was given. I saw me walk on the treadmill with purpose and with strength, carrying my head high and my body upright. I felt myself give all my energy into each and every element of the test. I imagined seeing a passing score and hearing the doctor tell me that I was approved.

The day of my physical fitness exam came.

We started the grueling process. I felt the burn in my lungs, the heaviness in my legs and arms. But I kept on and gave everything I had.

The process lasted about 30 minutes and I dare say these were the most challenging minutes of my life.

After I was finished, I went home to wait for the results.

It was August 27, 2003 when I heard the news. I had passed the physical fitness test by 2 points.

I cried in sheer joy as I bowed my head and thanked the Lord for this blessing. That same day, I was put on the National Transplant Registry.

I knew there was a wait period for me to get my new lungs and I was determined to look at the wait as another challenge to conquer. I was really weak, but I knew without a doubt that everything was going to be okay.

Just two days later, a miracle happened.

I got the call on August 29, 2003 and was told to be at UAB in two hours. The medical team had found a donor.

Not only had the team found a donor, but unlike most cases where the donor could be thousands of miles away, this donor had been on life support for a week, was a match with my rare blood type and was in the same city as UAB.

My doctors warned me that it might be a dry run – the process for an organ transplant is that all of the organs must be harvested in a specific order, there were time constraints to get the organs out without doing damage and there might be unforeseen health problems with the lungs. Plus, the family was still deciding if they would stand by the wishes of the donor to only donate the lung and heart or to donate the whole body to help others.

Tammy and I hung up the phone and held each other in our arms. We were in shock – the news was almost unbelievable. We were so excited, nervous, scared – all the emotions were jumbled together. But, my lungs were here and I had a chance.

Tammy started grabbing our overnight bags, oxygen tank and other necessities and started loading the car. I watched her, tormented because I wanted to help her but I was so weak that I could barely stand.

She was going back and forth to the car, when a man stopped by and asked her if he could help load the car. Tammy gratefully said yes and he came into our home to help carry things to the car.

On his last trip out of the apartment, he stopped to talk with me. I remember feeling a great sense of peace overcome me as he looked me straight in the eye and said, "**Everything is going to be alright with you, Jake.**" He left the house and finished placing the last load in the car.

When Tammy turned around to thank him, he was gone. The kind man was nowhere to be found. We wanted to say thank you for his help because those moments really were a matter of life and death. We spent a few minutes to check at the apartment complex office to see if anyone with this name lived there.

There was no one with that name registered at our complex.

To this day, I firmly believe that this man was an angel sent from God to tell me that everything was going to be okay. I knew at this time – and do to this day, with undeniable commitment, that the Lord is with us every step of the way.

And I knew I would be fine.

The Lord was in my life. I could feel His arms around me and I could hear His whisper as He lovingly told me before I entered the surgical transplant that I would be fine.

The rest of the details of that day in time were all a blur. I remember the drive from Atlanta to Birmingham and remember speeding as fast as humanly possible. Under normal circumstances, the drive takes two-and-a-half hours – we only had two hours to get there to be in time for the lungs.

I was never worried. I was feeling overwhelmed and anxious, but I knew it would all work out.

Tammy's family was waiting for us at UAB. I desperately wanted to see Mom and my brother, Paul, before I went in, but they did not make it in time before I had to be admitted.

As I was being wheeled into surgery, I lost consciousness several times. My carbon dioxide (CO_2) level was way over 100. Normal CO_2 levels are 30-40 mm, with 45 mm being the upper limit. Once levels go above 45 mm, it can lead to respiratory failure and death. I remember being woken up by the surgical team slapping me to get me back to consciousness before I went into the operating room. I still had peace and knew everything was going to be fine.

I still remember calling out to my wife and her family, "Peace! I will see you in a couple of days!"

My surgery lasted 15 hours.

During these precious moments, when most patients are deep in a state of unconsciousness, I had three visions. I didn't tell anyone about these visions for moths, because it scared me. Each revelation felt so, so real.

In the first vision, I was playing soccer. I was in the game and every time I got passed the ball, I'd get hit and a bone would break. There was no one else to play, so I had to keep playing. I kept getting hit over and over again. Bones were breaking and shattering, but I had to keep playing. Finally, I finished the game and I had to go to the hospital.

The first vision transitioned to the second vision … there were many playing cards, laid out in front of me. It looked like there were millions laying there. I had to match the cards with their pairs, like in the card game of Match. I remember feeling overwhelmed, like I was never going to be able to do this. I felt like giving up. But I kept at it and soon, I was down to the last four cards, then the last two cards … and as soon as I finished matching them, the third vision started.

I was in a black hole when all of a sudden, these doors started opening. They banged open – it was so loud in my head, you can't even imagine how loud it was.

Boom! Boom! Boom!

There were so many of them.

Each door opened and with every opened door, came a bright light. It grew closer and closer, and brighter and brighter.

I knew that I was either going to die … or I was coming back.

Overwhelming love and peace wrapped their wings around me.

And that's when I woke up. I came back.

It was a transition point in my life. I knew I was protected by God's love and in the depths of my soul, I knew everything was going to be all right.

I've had out of body experiences before. There were times that I was so sick, before the double lung transplants, that I should have been dead. The carbon dioxide (CO_2) in my body had built up to levels that were off the chart. During these times of the CO_2 build up, I would hallucinate. I'd do things – like one time, I bought furniture when I was so ill – that I didn't remember. Those times were the times that I knew I was dying.

This time was not about death.

This time, it was about life…about facing challenges and overcoming them so that I could get to the next phase in my life and my next calling … it was about God … and about witnessing His loving hand in my life and knowing that He lives.

My first memory after surgery was hearing Paul's voice. I was so thirsty. My mouth was so dry. I still had the tracheal tube in my throat, and I remember begging Paul for ice chips. He didn't want to give me the ice chips because he was afraid it would hurt me. I told him it wouldn't hurt and that I would be okay if he just gave me some relief from my thirst. He didn't want to do it, but he did anyway. Seeing his face and feeling his love meant the world to me. I knew then that I had made it safely through the journey and was surrounded by my family.

You know something? I was still thirsty days later, when the nurses were about the pull the tracheal tube from my lungs... and Paul was still by my side, ice chips in hand.

Post-Transplant

One of my first post-operation experiences was the amazing feeling of being able to take a FULL breath of air! For the *first* time in my life, I felt both lungs fill with air! I felt like I could inhale forever and ever.

I will never forget that fantastic moment.

My recovery time was very short. While double-lung transplant recipients can spend anywhere between three to six months recovering, I was only in the hospital for a total of ten days. I'm not saying that it was easy – while I was in the hospital and in rehabilitation, it felt like I had to learn how to walk all over again. I had been so sick for so long that I had not used my muscles for nearly a year and a half. But I met each day with an iron will to exercise, to become strong again and to recover as fast as I could.

I attribute my quick recovery to many things. My faith in God gave me the courage to continue, my mind focused solely on recovery and my heart was devoted to putting in whatever effort was necessary.

I wanted to be strong right then and there. I wanted to recover.

One day, during my recovery, Tammy and I had a short, but meaningful conversation. I remember telling her, "Hurry up! You need to get on this train because I'm about to take off!" And that's exactly how I felt! I knew that I was about to flourish.

I will always remember how she supported me and was my biggest cheerleader. Tammy's love and effort is one of the main reasons my recovery was so successful and so quick. I will never forget that and I will always love her for that.

After being discharged from the hospital, the medical team required me to live in Birmingham for a period of time so they could monitor my progress. Normally, an organ recipient has to live in the vicinity of the hospital for two months. I did so well that I was able to move home to Atlanta a month early.

My first birthday was Tuesday, August 15, 1972.

I was born again on Friday, August 29, 2003. I know the Lord had plans for me and that is why I was given a second chance. I consider August 29 my real birthday.

As I looked forward to the future, I knew that another chapter in my life had been written and that a blank page lay before me to write more chapters in the book of my life.

Death Knocks a 2nd Time

The year following my double lung transplant was a time of great growth for me. I started to rebuild my mind and my body. Each day, I woke up to the joyous thought, "*I can BREATHE*! It's amazing!"

I dedicated a portion of each day to exercise, meditation and prayer. I grew stronger with each passing day and my rehabilitation started moving at a faster pace.

My surgery was on August 29, 2003 and I was back at work at Camp Twin Lakes less than ten months later, with a 'return to work date' of May 29, 2004. It was fantastic and one of the happiest days in my life.

Although many things in my life were on the right track, I realized with a sinking heart that my marriage was coming to an end.

I believe God brings people in and out of our lives for specific reasons. Sometimes, the relationship lasts a lifetime and sometimes, it is time bound. More often than not, we don't know the reason we are brought together, but eventually the reasons are revealed. Tammy and I were meant to be together for a period of time; God sent her to me to care for me and help me get to the next stage.

In my darkest hours, Tammy stood by me and did everything she could for me. But, the experience took its toll on her. I sensed her exhaustion and started noticing small changes. For a long time, I couldn't put my finger on exactly what was going on, but thing were different.

One day, I realized that I was out of my meds sooner than I should be. I was religious about taking the exact dosage at the exact times; after all, my life depended on it.

Slowly, I understood what was causing the changes in Tammy. In order to cope with the ongoing, day to day stress of being my caregiver, she had turned to narcotics and was using my medicine as a crutch.

We talked about it, but unfortunately, the damage to our relationship was done. Tammy's dependency on narcotics was something she could not walk away from and there was no way I could take away the hurt that my care had inflicted on her.

When I returned from camp that summer, we both knew our marriage was over and decided to part ways. We divorced when I was 32 years old

With all of my heart, I appreciate everything she did for me and can only hope that I gave her something she needed in return. I would not be here today without her support. I know God brought us together for a specific amount of time for specific reasons.

I mourned the death of our marriage, but also kept my sights on the fact that God had given me a second chance – He gave me LIFE. I embraced this gift and pursued life to the max, living each moment to the fullest! I was catching up for lost time when I was sick and there was no way I was going to waste even one second.

I looked back at the many surgeries, the countless procedures, the never-ending prodding and poking, the violations from the medical community, the tons of doctors and the endless pain I had gone through so far. I knew my success was because of my mental focus and commitment to my health. My mind was given to me by God. I just recognized the gift and learned how to use it, to sharpen that God-given talent to focus on beating all the odds and overcoming the obstacles in front of me.

Physically, I never felt better. I worked out, ate properly, continued with the tube feedings and kept myself hydrated. I met with my medical team as scheduled. The doctors were amazed at my progression. All of the labs and tests were positive every step of the way and showed that I was healing. I was rejection-free, meaning that my body had fully accepted and adapted to the new lungs as my own. All my test and lab results came back positive, with continuous improvement on a regular, consistent basis.

Mentally, I felt free. I made it a deliberate decision to enjoy every day and live as if it were my last. I did not allow anything to hold me back.

The summer of 2005 was my fourth and final summer working at Camp Twin Lakes. I had been divorced for a while and met Ashley, a summer romance that blossomed into my second real relationship. I know now that our attraction was superficial and not a real love relationship, but I wanted to live every instant and dating her was a part of it. We enjoyed each other's company and had some great times.

Travel was a great joy of ours. One trip was to the Rocky Mountains in Colorado over Valentine's Day. Ashley made all the arrangements, just told me to be available on a certain day and be dressed and ready to hike. We pulled into the parking area at the base of the mountain and began to hike. As we climbed over the top of one of the mountains, we came to a secluded area and I discovered a surprise. She had set a blanket out for us, with all the picnic trimmings. I remember looking at her and feeling so happy, spending time with someone I enjoyed and having the strength and ability to climb the Rocky Mountains – such a far cry from 2003, when I could barely walk.

I continued to work out harder and push myself further, both mentally and physically, than I had ever done before.

One way to show the world – and more importantly, myself – was to do something incredibly remarkable.

I decided to run a half marathon!

I reworked my training regimen to meet the endurance and strength requirements of the race. It was tough work, but I was committed whole-heartedly and loved the sense of working toward my goal.

In the spring of 2009, I competed in and finished my first half-marathon! It was such a tremendous accomplishment for me. I still celebrate that cherished memory and feel it is a testament that we can do anything we set our minds to and believe with all our hearts that we can do.

2009, Atlanta GA, Competing in the ING Half Marathon

A couple of weeks after the race, I took on a new job at Piedmont Park Conservancy, a non-profit organization that works with the City of Atlanta to preserve the historical Piedmont Park. They offer multiple community programs and my role was a Counselor for the children's activities.

After camp ended that summer, I went to the park and stood there. I felt amazing – so strong and so good; I felt **indestructible**. I felt like the man of steel.

What I didn't realize at the time was that I had lost sight and appreciation of what God had given me. I was swept up in the superficial world, losing sight of God's grace and immersing myself in ego, with a big head puffed with the self-importance to go with it.

I have learned that what God gives, He can take away in an instant. And He can bring us to our knees in a microsecond, humbling us so that we can get back on the path of light.

Within a short time after my visit to the park, I came down with a little cough. I felt something was wrong in my lungs, the heavy feeling of being sick that I had not felt in seven years since the transplant returned. I was quickly and soundly knocked off my high horse and didn't understand why. All of the work I had done mentally and physically was about to be torn down over the next couple of years.

During the same time frame, Ashley and I started having problems and began drifting apart. Our relationship became very strained; she had only known me in my bright days of strength and had never seen me when I was sick.

As hard as it was to accept, it became obvious to me that she didn't want to live a life with someone who had a severe lifelong illness like CF. I was getting sicker day by day and our problems increased in direct proportion to my illness.

I started going into the hospital more and more frequently. The doctors couldn't figure out what was wrong with my lungs or why I was having a relapse.

After multiple hospital admissions, the tests revealed that I had Mycobacterium Avium Complex (MAC), a non-contagious infection of the lungs related to the tuberculosis germ. It is a disease of the lobes that is very hard to treat and cure because of the difficulty in getting the medicine to the infected nodules or cavity.

In addition to MAC, my lab results started indicating that there were issues with my kidneys. The level of cystatin C, a blood component used for early-stage detection of kidney disease, was high and climbing.

The doctors were concerned and ordered more tests. Once the results were in, I received a call.

I was diagnosed with kidney failure, also known as acute renal failure.

The wind was knocked out of me.

Kidney failure is a terrible condition. Basically, it means that your kidneys suddenly stop working to remove waste products from the blood stream and can no longer balance minerals, water and salt. The by-product is that waste products, electrolytes and fluids build up in your body, causing serious problems that can be deadly.

I became depressed and angry. I was obsessed with all the hard work that I had done, all that I had gained and all that I had lost. My mental clarity once again blurred and my mental toughness lost ground as well.

A major contributor to the kidney failure was a side effect of the medications I had been taking since 2003, when I had the double lung transplant. While I knew the meds were very toxic to the kidneys, I had to take the medication to live. It was a damning catch 22.

By December of 2009, my second real relationship that I'd ever had in my life was over.

I was pretty much on my own from the age of 37 to 39. I found support and solace with my family. Mom, Paul and my sister Elizabeth, plus a few select friends (Brad, Ernest and Adam), were in my life. They helped me in so many ways – from being there to talk to when I needed a shoulder to cry on, to bringing meals, to helping me stay on track and re-focus my life.

I continued to pray to God. I asked Him why I was now faced with kidney failure, after I had been subjected to so much through my life. I humbled myself before Him, stripping my ego and really listening to His voice. I came to understand why I had been knocked down. I had allowed myself to be swept up in my own arrogance, taking full credit for my healthy and speedy recovery and losing sight that my healing was possible through God's will and grace.

As I realized the truth, I bowed my head and made a solemn vow to God. I promised that I would always put Him first and to never allow myself to get caught up in the superficial again. I made humility my priority and appreciation for the gift of life and His love as part of my life's philosophy.

God heard my prayers. I did not realize it then, but He set into motion a series of events that allowed His will to be done through me. His plan was to prepare my family and give them the strength they needed to endure what was going to happen in the not so distant future.

My illness progressed. This time, in the depths of my illness, I never lost my faith or my focus. I knew why I had gotten sick and understood why it was happening.

Time continued and gradually got worse. My hospital visits became more frequent with the kidney problems.

I reflected on my life since the double lung transplant, returning to my outlook that my life was divided by chapters. These past few years – filled with running a half-marathon, maintaining a faithful workout routine, eating properly and developing my inner focus and control - it was all training to gear up for the upcoming war I was going to face.

The war was on the horizon.

Top: 2003 with Tammy, before the double lung transplant
Bottom: Getting sicker before the transplant

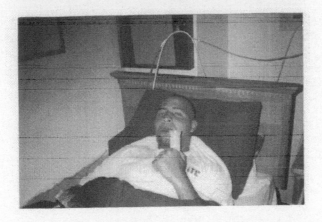

Top: Sunset at the top of Rockefeller Center, NYC, 2009

Bottom: In the CF Center, Atlanta GA, 1997

Top: Hiking in 2008

Bottom: Hiking in 2005

26 years old, Florida

3rd Time's a Charm

Kidney failure is one of those diseases that can take a long time to manifest or it can come on quickly and knock you to your knees in an instant.

I was 38 years old when my kidneys went into failure. My illness progressed very quickly.

At first, I felt a little off, like something wasn't quite right. I continued to eat well and exercise daily. But my strength was quickly disappearing and I had very little energy. I lost a lot of weight, was feverish, and had a constant pain in my side. I was always tired and instinctually knew my health was declining.

Even though I consciously knew I was sick and needed more intensive medical treatment, I put off talking to the doctors about my kidney problems. It's not that I was in denial; my mind just wasn't ready to openly admit it. I was not at the point where I could focus on developing a plan of attack. I knew in my heart that when it was time, my heart, mind and faith would let me know.

During this time, my Mom was still married to my father. I had lived away from my parents for more than a decade and although I visited, the trips were not very often. I remember the overwhelming feelings of negativity that washed over me every time I went to see them. My dad was still mentally and emotionally abusive to my Mom – always cutting her down and never a kind word to say. Mom gained a lot of weight, extra pounds put on to protect her from the onslaught of psychic assaults with which my father constantly bombarded her.

One day, I went to visit and knew within my heart that I could no longer stand by and watch my Mom as such a victim. I sat her down and told her that, for my own mental and physical health, I was not going to come back to the house because of my father.

I shared with her that one truth I had learned from my experiences that life itself is a precious gift too short to sacrifice joy and good to be around negativity. I told her that I loved her and knew she didn't have a bad bone in her body; that she was filled with goodness and love. But, I also told her that she was in a mental prison –she could not see the damage caused by the relationship with my father. She was a victim … but she was allowing herself to remain a victim.

There were tears in my eyes. With a heavy heart, I gave her an ultimatum. I could not be around or witness the dysfunctional relationship. I had to distance myself from it because my health and my very life literally depended on being around positive energy and people. She had to choose a relationship with me or with him. I simply could not accept being around my father and I could not accept seeing her in a relationship with a man that did not value nor respect her.

Once the words came out of my mouth, I was terrified. I was scared to death that Mom would be angry and not understand why I had to take this stance. I was afraid that she would reject me and choose a life of torment. But I trusted my gut. I had faith that I was supposed to talk with her and tell her these things. I prayed to God that the right words would come out and the message would be received with the spirit in which it was intended.

For a moment, Mom was absolutely quiet.

Then, she responded and I breathed a sigh of relief.

She did not get angry. Instead, Mom listened to what I was saying and made the decision to leave a marriage that had been killing her for so many years.

As she started a new chapter in her life, she transformed herself. She lost more than 80 lbs., changed her eating habits, started regular exercise and re-energized herself. She broke free from the chains of the mental prison and started believing in herself. She grew stronger – both mentally and physically – with each passing day. She started to flourish in her job and is now quite successful in the insurance industry. She has her own home, which is beautiful, and she's transformed from a victim to a thriving survivor.

My hero, Mom

One night, in September 2011, I was talking with Carmen, my current girlfriend. I had been praying a lot and listening to my body. During our conversation, I felt God reveal to me that the time had come. I told Carmen it was time for me to start the process for a kidney transplant. As we talked, it became very apparent to me that the events of my life – learning how to walk again after the double lung transplant, running the half marathon, understanding what I needed to do (and just as importantly, having the strength to do it) each day to keep my physical and mental strength up, falling away from God and finding Him again, getting sick with kidney failure, inspiring my Mom to change her life – all of these things led up to one point in time: to get my kidney transplant.

Dialysis, an artificial process of removing waste and water from the blood stream, is the traditional method of treating patients with kidney failure. But I knew within my heart that I would not need it.

As Carmen and I talked, she asked me who I thought could be a donor. The answer was there – I knew my Mom would be the donor and knew that she was healthy enough now to be able to give her kidney to me, should she be willing. I also felt that the time would go quickly – the required battery of tests for me and Mom would be fast.

A calm sense came over me as I heard God whisper to me that both Mom and my experience in the surgery room and our post-operative recovery would be fine and would go without a problem.

The day of my transplant arrived.

March 29, 2012.

The night before the operation, I looked myself in the mirror. I told myself that the pain and sickness from the kidney failure would be over soon. I gazed deeply into my own eyes, into the depths of my soul, so that I would remember what I felt like before the surgery and what I looked like. I want to always remember what that sickness felt like so I would always know the drastic change I would feel once the surgery was complete.

The next morning, Mom and I prayed together. We asked God to guide our medical team and to be with us during our recovery.

We were wheeled into the operating room together. I remember holding her hand and looking her in the eye, thanking her for being there for me.

Three hours later, we woke up in the recovery room to find that the procedure went off without a hitch. We were both doing fine and were exactly where we needed to be for a solid recovery.

I thank my Mom for the gift of life. Not only did she bring me into this world, but through her unconditional love, she gave me life a second time through sacrificing her own kidney.

Throughout it all, I had a constant belief that the Lord would make everything turn out fine and work out for the best.

And He has.

Looking Forward

At the time of this book, I'm 41 years old.

It's been a little more than six months since the kidney transplant.

I am so grateful for everything I have. Carmen and I are still together and I really do feel she is my soul mate. She has my best interests at heart and she truly loves me. And I love her back.

Earlier in life, I made the conscious decision not to have children because of my CF. But the Lord saw fit to bless me with a family anyway. Arie, Carmen's daughter, has accepted me into her family.

My health is good. I keep up with the required tests and labs; the results continue to be positive. I feel strong, I work out, I eat healthy and I respect my body for the temple it is. It's amazing to me to think that it was just a year since I had the surgery.

It feels like decades ago, like another lifetime.

I look back now and wonder what my purpose is here on Earth. For all accounts, death has knocked three times on my door. I could have died so many times … yet I live. I've endured indescribable pain, withstood significant health challenges, persevered immeasurable mental stress and survived monumental medical procedures. My life started with a diagnosis of Cystic Fibrosis, I had a double lung transplant and a kidney transplant.

Incredible experiences have taken place in my life, and my life is nothing short of a miracle by the grace of God.

I have met amazing people because of my medical problems. And although I am strong now, I know that the journey of life will always be filled with medical tests and procedures – but I have life. And these events of my life led me to where I am now, with a woman I love and a little girl I adore. I live a happy life with them and give them as much love and support as I can.

Every morning, I look up to the sky and thank God for another day. I rejoice in life and live each day to the fullest. I realize now that all the events in my life were part of a path I had to follow. This path was filled with heartache, pain, joy and triumph – and every step of the journey prepared me to deal with what came next in my life. It made me stronger and gave me courage. It made me confident that I can – and will be able to – deal with anything.

I believe there is a plan for me. If there wasn't, I would not be here today.

I also believe there is a plan for you.

I know that my life is a testimony not only to God, but to the power of the mind. You really can conquer many things by focusing on what you have to get through, no matter how big or small the challenge. Whether it's finding a new job or living a purposeful life despite a significant health challenge, we each have the power within us to focus, to find the inner strength and to conquer the challenge.

We all face challenges and hardships. These experiences are part of our life to test our strength and to build our character.

When I set out to write my story and share the experiences I've been through, I wanted to inspire, to be a positive beacon of light and encouragement. If I can help just one person dealing with any roadblock, either medically or other everyday life problems, then I've fulfilled my calling.

If I can offer you some insight I've learned along the way, some guidance, I offer you this:

- No matter what you are facing today, no matter how big it seems, I know you can do it.

- I believe in your power to reach into the depths of your being and find the strength to fight.

- Avoid feeling sorry for yourself. You are here for a reason. Your experiences are part of a bigger plan.

- Hold on to hope and never give up in life.

- Stay focused.

- Stay positive.

- Give it everything you can.

- Appreciate the details of your life. The magic is in simplicity.

- Dedicate yourself to finding a solution.

- Believe, with all your might, it is possible to succeed.

- Have faith in God.

- Demonstrate your commitment and belief by putting in the hard work to solve the problems. The Lord will walk with you to see that problems get resolved.

- And give back. That's important. Giving back is your way to show God your appreciation.

You can do it.

I promise.

Jake

Made in the USA
San Bernardino, CA
22 January 2016